Guess What!

Student's Book 6

American English

Susannah Reed with **Kay Bentley**

Series Editor: Lesley Koustaff

CAMBRIDGE
UNIVERSITY PRESS

Contents

Seasons and weather

1 CD1 02 **Listen and look.**

2 CD1 03 **Listen and repeat. Then match.**

a fall   **b** drought   **c** flood   **d** monsoon   **e** spring
f storm   **g** summer   **h** thunder and lightning   **i** winter

3 CD1 04 Think **Listen and say** *yes* **or** *no*. **Then ask and answer.**

Is the weather in the spring cold and snowy?   No!

4 My World **Is the weather today usual for the season? Ask and answer.**

5 **Read and listen. Then match.**

Where did you go on summer vacation?

1 I went to stay with my cousins in Colombia. It was hot and sunny. We went to the beach, and we went bodyboarding. It was great.
Josh

2 I visited my pen pal in India. It was the monsoon season, and there was a lot of rain. We played soccer in the rain. It was fun!
Luis

3 I stayed with my mom's friends in Bali. It was very windy, but there weren't any storms or rain. We went to a kite festival. It was fantastic.
Nicola

6 **Match the questions and answers.**

1 Where did Josh go on summer vacation?
2 What did Josh do there?
3 What was the weather like in India?
4 Was there a storm in Bali?
5 Did the children enjoy their vacation?

a He went bodyboarding.
b No, there wasn't.
c He went to Colombia.
d Yes, they did.
e It was rainy.

7 **My World** **Ask and answer.**

Where did you go on summer vacation?

I went to Spain.

Focus!
What was the weather like?
It was hot and sunny.
Was there a storm?
Yes, there was. / No, there wasn't.

Say it!

8 **Does the end of the question go up or down? Listen and repeat.**

Was there a storm? ↗   Did you enjoy your vacation? ↗

9 **What are they talking about? Listen and choose.**

a a drought   b a storm   c a monsoon

10 **Listen again and practice.**

Alex: What's your scariest memory, Carla?

Carla: When I was six, I went to Florida on vacation.

Alex: In the United States? That sounds great!

Carla: Well, wait and see. The weather was great when we arrived, but then there was a bad storm.

Alex: Oh, no!

Carla: It was really windy, and it rained and rained. Then there was a flood in our hotel.

Alex: How awful!

Carla: Yes! We had to leave our hotel by boat. It was really scary.

Alex: Poor you.

> **Focus!**
>
> **When** I was six, I went to Florida.
> The weather was great **when** we arrived.

11 **World** **Read and match. Then make sentences that are true for you.**

Memories

1 When we went on vacation,

2 I met my best friend

3 When we got our new puppy,

4 My brother Rufus was born

5 When we moved to our new house,

a when she came to my school.

b it ate my mom's new shoe.

c I found a big snake in our yard.

d when I was five.

e we saw turtles on the beach.

> When we went on vacation, I went windsurfing on a lake.

12 **Go to page 102. Listen and repeat the chant.**

Skills: *Listening and speaking*

Let's start! What's your favorite season? Why?

14 (CD1 11) **Who's speaking? Listen and say the names.**

Luca

Stacie

Palin

Elise

15 (CD1 11) **Listen again and complete the sentences.**

1 Elise is from _____ .
2 Palin's favorite season is _____ .
3 _____ likes going to summer camp.
4 Stacie went _____ on a lake last summer.
5 Luca _____ skiing.

16 (CD1 12) **Talk Time** **Plan a trip with a friend.**

Where would you like to go next summer?

I'd like to go to …

Good idea. What's the weather like in … then?

It's …

OK. Can we … ?

Yes, and we can …

Skills: *Reading and writing*

Look below! **Where did Joe go on his school trip?**

17 **Read and listen.**

The Sonoran Desert
by Joe

Last spring, our class went to the Sonoran Desert in Mexico. It's one of the biggest and hottest deserts in North America. We went in the spring because the summer is too hot.

We stayed there for a week. When we arrived, it was sunny and windy. On our first day, we visited the Altar sand dunes. Some of the dunes are more than one hundred meters high. They were beautiful, and we enjoyed climbing on them.

It's very dry in the Sonoran Desert. There are lots of cacti, but there aren't usually many other plants. We were lucky because on our second day, it started to rain. When it rains, the desert changes because flowers can grow. We went hiking on the last day, and there were beautiful flowers everywhere!

18 **Read again and say *true* or *false*.**

1 The Sonoran Desert is in Brazil.
2 It isn't a big desert.
3 The desert is very hot in winter.
4 The sand dunes are very high.
5 It never rains in the Sonoran Desert.
6 Flowers can grow in the spring in the Sonoran Desert.

Your turn!

Think about a class trip.
Where did you go?
What season was it?
What was the weather like?
What did you do?

Now write about it in your notebook.

What do the shadows in a painting tell us?

1 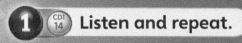 **Listen and repeat.**

shadow

light from above

light from the side

2 **Watch the video.**

3 CD1 15 **Read and listen.**

Artists use shadows to show different seasons and times of day. To show summer, artists often paint short shadows. This is because the Sun is high in the sky in summer, and when the light comes from above, it makes short shadows.
In winter, the Sun is lower in the sky. The light comes from the side and makes longer shadows.

Artists also paint long shadows to show the morning or the evening and short shadows to show midday.

The shadows in paintings can also tell us where the Sun is in the sky. When the shadows are on the right of the objects, the Sun is on the left. When the shadows are in front, the Sun is behind.

Guess What!

Shadows aren't just black. They're darker in the center and lighter on the outside.

4 **Answer the questions.**

1 What's different about shadows in summer paintings and in winter paintings?
2 Why do we see long shadows in winter paintings?
3 Are shadows shorter in the morning or at midday?
4 Look at the painting on page 12. Where is the Sun?

5 **Which season would you like to paint?**

Project

6 Paint a picture that shows a season. Write about it and say where the Sun and shadows are.

This is my spring painting. The shadows are really short. We can't see the Sun in the painting, but we know the Sun is on the left because the shadows are on the right.

1 Camping

1 (CD1 16) **Listen and look.**

2 (CD1 17) **Listen and repeat. Then match.**

a blanket   b bowl   c cup   d map   e plate   f backpack
g sleeping bag   h tent   i flashlight   j water bottle

3 (CD1 18) (Think) **Listen and guess the words. Then practice with a friend.**

You stay in this when you're camping.   A tent!

4 (My World) **What do you need when you go camping? Ask and answer.**

5 CD1 19 **Read and listen.**

I had a strange weekend. I went camping with my family because we wanted to sleep outside, but my dad forgot to take the tent! We tried to make a tent with a blanket, but it wasn't very good. We were cold. We needed to make a fire, but we didn't have any firewood. Then it started to rain, and our sleeping bags got wet. We had to come home. We still want to sleep outside someday.
Zoe

Focus!

We wanted **to sleep** outside.
My dad forgot **to take** the tent.
We tried **to make** a tent.

6 Think **Read, complete, and order the sentences.**

want/sleep   try/make   start/rain   need/make   forget/take   have/go

a   They _____ a tent with a blanket because they _____ their tent.
b   Their sleeping bags got wet because it _____ .
c   They _____ a fire because they were cold.
d   Zoe's family was excited because they _____ in a tent.
e   They _____ home because they got wet.

7 My World **Make true and false sentences about yourself. Then talk to a friend.**

I forgot _____ this morning.
I want _____ after school today.
I need _____ on Saturday.
I tried _____ yesterday.
I had _____ last week.

I forgot to brush my teeth this morning.

False!

Say it!

8 CD1 20 CD1 21 **Which words sound the strongest? Listen and repeat.**

We **wanted** to **sleep** in a **tent**.   We **needed** to **make** a **fire**.

What does Pedro have to do? Listen and choose.

a put up the tent   b wash the cups and bowls
c cook the dinner

Emma

Pedro

 Listen again and practice.

Teacher: OK, everyone, come and help me, please.
Emma: Yes, of course. What do we have to do?
Teacher: Emma, put up the tent, please. And Pedro …
Pedro: Yes?
Teacher: Please wash the cups and bowls.
Pedro: Aww! Can I put up the tent?
Teacher: No, Pedro. I asked Emma to put up the tent.
Pedro: Can I help cook the dinner?
Teacher: No, Pedro. What did I ask you to do?
Pedro: You asked me to wash the cups and bowls.

Focus!

What did I **ask** you **to do**?
You **asked** me **to wash**
the cups and bowls.

11 **My World** **Whisper an instruction to a friend. Then mime and guess.**

cook dinner

wash the cups

carry the backpack

find the map

carry the water bottle

put up the tent

look for the flashlight

turn off the flashlight

pass me a blanket

Please carry the backpack.

What did she ask me to do?

She asked you to carry the backpack.

 Go to page 102. Listen and repeat the chant.

13 CD1 24 **Read and listen.**

Skills: *Listening and speaking*

Let's start! Do you like camping? Why or why not?

14 CD1 25 **Where do Rosie and Tilly want to go camping? Listen and say the letter.**

Sleep like a bird.

Wake up to mountain views.

Watch for dolphins at night.

15 CD1 25 **Listen again and answer the questions.**

1 Does Tilly like mountains?
2 Is the tree tent in a campsite?
3 Can you go hiking in the national park?
4 Are there showers close to the tent on the ocean?
5 What do Rosie and Tilly need to take with them?

16 CD1 26 **Talk Time** **Plan a camping trip with a friend.**

Should we go camping?

Yes, great! Let's go to …

Who should we go with?

Why don't we go with … ?

OK. Let's take …

Yes, and I'll take …

Skills: *Reading and writing*

 Look below! **What does Ben Taylor do?**

17 **Read and listen.**

Camping on ice

Ben Taylor makes movies about animals. We asked him to describe his favorite movie-making experience.

"Last November, I had to make a movie about emperor penguins in Antarctica. I stayed on a boat, but one night I camped outside.

It was very cold. I had to have a very warm sleeping bag and a special tent, but I didn't need to take a flashlight. November is early summer in Antarctica, and it doesn't get dark.

Antarctica isn't quiet at night. You can hear the wind, and sometimes you can hear noisy penguins. You can hear the ice, too! Ice makes a strange sound when it moves.

When I woke up the next morning, there was a family of emperor penguins near my tent. I filmed them for two hours. It was so exciting I forgot to have breakfast!"

18 **Read again and correct the sentences.**

1 Ben went to Antarctica in January.
2 He had to make a movie about elephant seals.
3 He camped on the ice for seven nights.
4 He had to take a sleeping bag and a flashlight.
5 November is a winter month in Antarctica.
6 He was bored by the penguins.

 Your turn!

Imagine you make movies about animals.
What animals would you like to make a movie about?
What do they do?

Now write about it in your notebook.

How do we **estimate** measurements?

1 CD1 28 Listen and repeat.

How long?

How heavy?

How much?

1 meter = 100 centimeters

1 kilogram = 1,000 grams

1 liter = 1,000 milliliters

2 Watch the video.

3 CD1 29 Read and listen.

How long is your sleeping bag? How heavy is your backpack? How much water is there in your water bottle? When we don't know and we can't measure something, we have to guess, or estimate, measurements.

To help us estimate, we can think about other objects we know. For example, Alice knows her tent is 4 kg. Her backpack feels a bit heavier. Alice estimates that her backpack is about 5 kg.

When we're estimating, we use words like *it's about …* or *it's more than … , but less than …* For example: *The tent is about 250 cm long.* Or: *The tent is more than 2 m long, but less than 3 m long.*

4 Answer the questions.

1 What units of measurement do we use to find out how long something is?
2 How many centimeters are there in 3 meters?
3 Why do we sometimes have to estimate measurements?
4 What words do we use when we estimate?

5 Which is more difficult to estimate, how tall or how heavy your friends are?

Guess What!

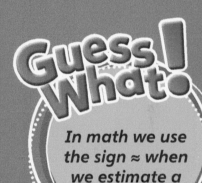

In math we use the sign ≈ when we estimate a number.

Project

6 **Find five objects. Estimate and then measure how long and how heavy each one is.**

Object	How long? Estimate	How long? Measurement	How heavy? Estimate	How heavy? Measurement
notebook	20 cm	30 cm	150 g	256 g
pencil case	25 cm	19 cm	250 g	180 g
eraser	4 cm	6 cm	40 g	16 g
pen	10 cm	15 cm	10 g	4 g
shoe	18 cm	21 cm	350 g	290 g

→ Workbook page 18

2 Talent show

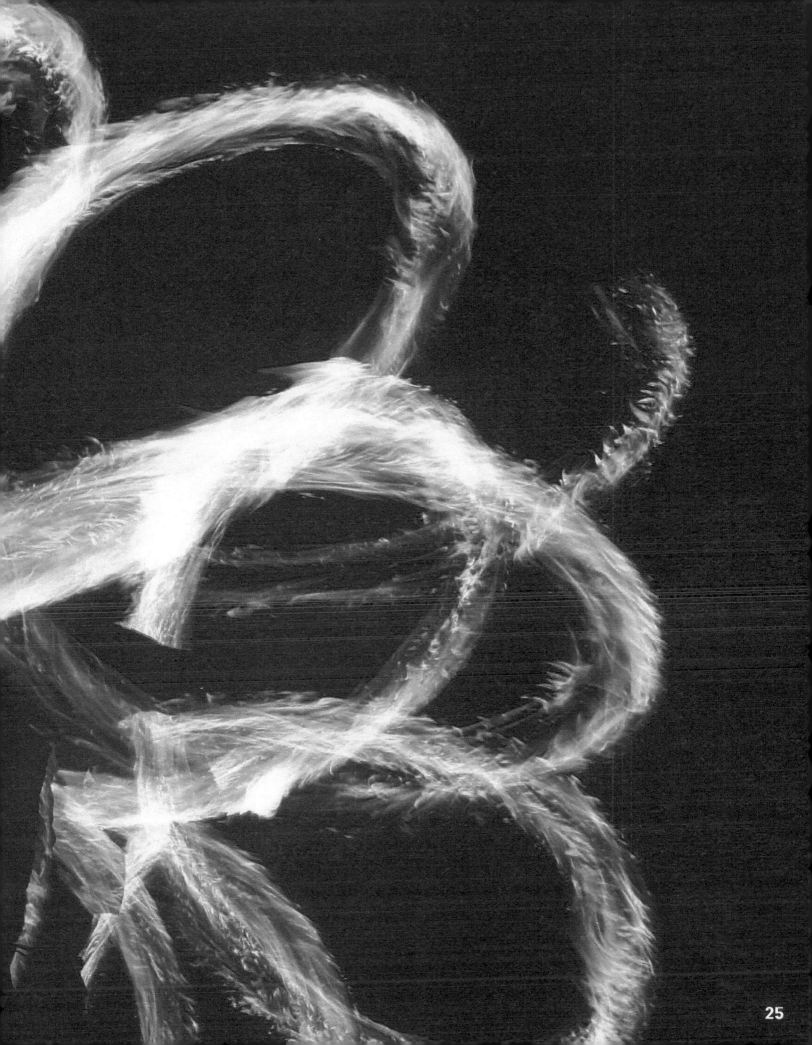

1 (CD1 30) Listen and look.

2 (CD1 31) Listen and repeat. Then match.

a do acrobatics   b do cartwheels   c do tricks   d juggle   e make sculptures
f paint portraits   g play instruments   h do street dancing   i read poetry   j tell jokes

3 (CD1 32) **Think** Listen and answer the questions. Then ask and answer.

Who's good at reading poetry?   The girl in picture 10.

4 **My World** What are you good at? Ask and answer.

5 (CD1 33) **Read, listen, and look.**

Paul, Zoe, and Jake are all good at street dancing. Paul is the best at street dancing. Zoe is better than Jake at street dancing, but she's worse than Paul. Jake is the worst at street dancing, but he's still good at it!

Focus!

good	better	the best
bad	worse	the worst

6 (Think) **Read and say the names. Then make more sentences.**

	Lily	Max	Ava	Oscar
Juggling	1st	2nd	3rd	4th
Doing cartwheels	2nd	3rd	4th	1st

1 She's better than Oscar at juggling, but she's worse than Max.
2 He's the worst at juggling.
3 He's better than Ava at doing cartwheels, but he's worse than Lily.
4 She's the best at juggling.
5 She's worse than Max at doing cartwheels.
6 He's better than Ava at doing cartwheels, but he's worse than her at juggling.

7 (My World) **Complete the riddle about a friend. Then ask the class to guess.**

I'm better than my friend at _____ , but I'm worse than him/her at _____ . My friend is the best in the class at _____ .

Say it!

8 (CD1 34) (CD1 35) **Which word sounds the strongest? Listen and repeat.**

Oscar isn't the best at juggling.　(Lily is the best at juggling.)

Oscar isn't the **best** at juggling.　(He's the worst at juggling.)

Oscar isn't the best at **juggling**.　(He's the best at doing cartwheels.)

9 **What did Alex make at the beach? Listen and choose.**

   a a sandcastle   **b** a sand portrait   **c** a sand sculpture

10 **Listen again and practice.**

Emma: What did you do on the weekend, Alex?

Alex: I went to the beach with my family. We had a sand sculpture competition. Look!

Emma: Cool! Who's the best at making sand sculptures in your family?

Alex: I am, I think. Look, it's a crocodile.

Emma: Really?

Alex: And this is my sister's.

Emma: Oh, yes!

Alex: Who's better at making sculptures, my sister or me?

Emma: Sorry, Alex. Your sister is.

> **Focus!**
>
> **Who's the best** at making sculptures? I am.
> **Who's better** at making sculptures, my sister or me? Your sister is.

11 **My World** **Choose the words. Then ask and answer.**

> better   best   worse   worst

1 Who's the b_____ at making sculptures in your family?

2 Who's b_____ at speaking English, your mom or your dad?

3 Who's w_____ at juggling, you or your best friend?

4 Who's the w_____ at telling jokes in your family?

5 Who's the b_____ at swimming in your class?

6 Who's the w_____ at cooking in your family?

7 Who's w_____ at singing, you or your best friend?

8 Who's b_____ at using a computer, you or your dad?

12 **Go to page 102. Listen and repeat the chant.**

13 Read and listen.

CD1 38

1 Follow the footprints to a canoe.
Inside it is your second clue.
North, south, east, or west.
This item always knows where's best.

2 Footprints?

Yes, look! Let's follow them.

3 They're very big footprints.

4 Here's the canoe! It's a compass. Of course! North, south, east, and west!

5 You go in front, Sofia. You're the best at reading the map.

I can paddle.

You take the compass, Ruby.

6 Slow down, Jack!

I can't! Which way do we go?

North. Go left!

7 We need to land over there.

Yes, but be careful of the hippos!

8 Good job, Jack.

Good job, all of us.

EMOCLEW

→ Workbook page 23

Value: Work together

29

Skills: *Listening and speaking*

Let's start! What type of street entertainment can you see in your country?

14 CD1 39 Which entertainers do Lia and Juan see? Listen and say the letters.

Watch some acrobats.

Find a 3-D picture.

Meet a giant puppet.

Try some juggling.

Talk to a statue.

15 CD1 39 Listen again and match.

1 The children say hello to …
2 The children decide to follow …
3 The children give money to …
4 Juan is better than Lia at …
5 Lia is better than Juan at …

a the puppet.
b juggling.
c the statue.
d dancing.
e the 3-D artist.

16 CD1 40 **Talk Time** Plan a street entertainment show with your friends.

I can … What can you do?

I can …

Great! And how about … ?

OK. … is the best at …

What can … do?

Why doesn't he/she … ?

Skills: *Reading and writing*

 What type of competition did Paola enter?

17 **Read and listen.**

Talent (by Paola)

Everyone's good at something,
In my family.
They all have a lot of talent,
Everyone but me!

My sister's good at painting,
She paints pictures of our town.
My brother's great at telling jokes,
He's the family clown.

My mom is the best singer,
And she plays the guitar, too.
And my dad is the best at cooking,
He makes a great barbecue.

But what can I be good at?
I'll ask my mom and dad,
"Am I good at anything,
Can I really be that bad?"

"Don't be silly," says my mom.
"Your talent's easy to see.
You're the best at writing,
You write great poetry!"

So now I feel quite happy,
And what I know is this,
We all have a talent,
Just find out what yours is!

18 **Read again and answer the questions.**

1 Who's the funniest in Paola's family?
2 Who's the best writer?
3 Who's the best at music?
4 Who makes very good food?
5 What does Paola like to write?
6 Who's very good at art?

Your turn!

Think about your family.
Is your family similar to or different from Paola's family? What are they good at? What are you good at?

Now write about it in your notebook.

What abilities do we need for **physical activities?**

1 CD1 42 Listen and repeat.

speed   strength   balance   stamina

2 Watch the video.

3 CD1 43 Read and listen.

Can you run, skate, or ride your bike fast? For these activities you need speed because you need to move your body very quickly.

Are you good at rock climbing? You need strength for this activity because you must have strong arms and legs to climb.

Can you stand on one leg without falling down? For this you need balance. Street dancers need good balance when they move on one leg or one arm.

Do you think you can run in a marathon? It isn't easy because we need to use our muscles for a long time. To run in a marathon, we need stamina.

Guess What!

Flamingos can balance on one leg when they sleep.

4 Answer the questions.

1 When do we need speed?
2 Why is it difficult to run in a marathon?
3 Which is more important when you do a cartwheel, stamina or balance?
4 Look at the picture on page 32. What abilities does the snowboarder need?

5 What would you like to have, better speed, strength, balance, or stamina?

Project

6 Find out about five popular physical activities in your country. Which abilities are the most important? Make a chart and then write about them.

Popular activities in my country

	1 bike racing	2 rock climbing	3 dancing	4 basketball	5 acrobatics
speed	✓			✓	
strength		✓			✓
balance	✓		✓	✓	✓
stamina		✓	✓		

In my country, bike racing, rock climbing, dancing, basketball, and acrobatics are popular. Speed is important for bike racing and basketball. People need strength for rock climbing and acrobatics. Balance is important for bike racing, dancing, basketball, and acrobatics. We need stamina for rock climbing and dancing.

Review Units 1 and 2

1 **Read, listen, and choose the words.**

Last **fall/winter**, I visited my friend Brad in New York. When I **arrive/arrived**, there was a **snowstorm/drought**. I was surprised because Brad asked **me/us** to go **camping/swimming**! But we didn't **camp/swim** outside in the **snow/monsoon**. We spent the night in a museum! We **had/forgot** to take **sleeping bags/tents**, a **water bottle/flashlight**, and a camera.

When the museum **closes/closed**, we explored in the dark with our **flashlights/cameras**. Then we watched a movie, and we slept under a **shark/whale**! Well, we **had/tried** to sleep, but we were too excited. We **told jokes/painted portraits**, and we did some **cartwheels/tricks**. Brad was the **best/worst** at **telling jokes/doing cartwheels**. We laughed a lot.

In the morning, we had breakfast, and then we went home to bed!

George

2 **Read again and answer the questions.**
1 Which season was it when George went to New York?
2 What was the weather like when George arrived?
3 Where did they go camping?
4 Did they need to take tents?
5 Was George the best at telling jokes?
6 Were they tired in the morning?

3 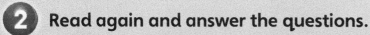 **Think of a visit to a friend. Ask and answer.**

Who did you visit?   Where did you go?
What season was it?   Where did you sleep?

4 **Write about your visit in your notebook.**

5 Play the game.

24 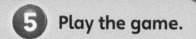 WELCOME TO THE TALENT SHOW

23 Go back to 19.

22 This morning, my teacher asked me to _____ .

21 Name five activities you are good at.

17 When I was _____ , I went to _____ on vacation.

18 Go back to 14.

19 yesterday? / weather / was / the / like / What

20 Go to 21.

16 Go to 17.

15 Who / at / is / best / painting / the / your / in / family?

14 Name five activities you can do on vacation.

13 Go back to 11.

9 flood / Was / fall? / last / a / there

10 Name six things you take when you go camping.

11 _____ is _____ than me at juggling.

12 Name four weather words.

8 _____ is the _____ in our class at doing cartwheels.

7 Go to 10.

6 Go back to 2.

5 your parents / to do / ask / What / last night? / did / you

1 Start here!

2 summer? / go / Where / last / you / did

3 This morning, I forgot to _____ .

4 Name four seasons.

Green
Make a question and answer it.

Yellow
Make a true sentence.

Blue
How many words can you remember?

3 International food

1 (CD1 45) **Listen and look.**

2 (CD1 46) **Listen and repeat. Then match.**

a curry   **b** dumplings   **c** fish and chips   **d** kebabs   **e** noodles
f paella   **g** rice and beans   **h** stew   **i** sushi   **j** tacos

3 (CD1 47) (Think) **Listen and suggest dishes. Then practice with a friend.**

I like fish and potatoes. I don't like rice.   Why don't you try fish and chips?

4 (My World) **Which of these dishes would you like to try? Ask and answer.**

5 (CD1 48) **Read and listen.**

I'm learning to cook international food with my Saturday club. Now my family wants me to cook dinner every night, and they usually want me to make different things.

Yesterday evening, my mom wanted me to make rice and beans, my dad wanted me to make pasta, and my sister wanted me to make sushi.

What can I do? I want them to cook dinner for me sometimes!

Andy

Focus!

My family **wants** me **to cook** dinner every night. I **want** them **to cook** dinner for me sometimes.

6 (Think) **Read and match. Then choose the words.**

1 She wants **her/him** to read a story.

2 They want **him/her** to play soccer.

3 They want **him/her** to buy fish and chips.

4 She wants **him/them** to make noodles for dinner.

5 He wants **you/her** to try some dumplings.

6 He wants **her/them** to go to bed.

7 (My World) **Think of three things you want people to do after school.**

I want Sally to come to my house.

I want my mom to make stew for dinner.

I want my brother to clean my room.

8 (CD1 49) **Go to page 102. Listen and repeat the chant.**

→ Workbook page 31

9 **What did Carla make? Listen and choose.**

a paella   b kebabs   c tacos

10 **Listen again and practice.**

Pedro: Hi, Carla. Where were you this morning?

Carla: I went to the supermarket to buy some rice.

Pedro: Some rice? Why did you buy rice?

Carla: I bought some rice to make paella. I had chicken and vegetables, but I didn't have any rice. The paella's for you, Pedro. Happy birthday!

Pedro: Thanks, Carla. I love paella.

Carla: I know!

> **Focus!**
>
> I went to the supermarket to buy some rice.
> I bought some rice to make a paella.

11 **My World** **Choose and make sentences. How many true sentences can you make?**

> the supermarket   the market
> the park a restaurant   a store
> the sports center   the movie theater

> buy   have   eat   play
> do   go   ride   watch

> Yesterday, I went to the sports center to do karate.

> On Saturday, my mom and dad went to a restaurant to have dinner.

Say it!

12  **Which words sound the strongest? Listen and repeat.**

I **went** to the **market** to **buy** some **rice**.

I **bought** some **rice** to **make paella**.

Skills: *Listening and speaking*

Let's start! Can you cook? Would you like to enter a cooking competition?

14 CD1 54 **How does Jake make his dish? Listen and order the pictures.**

a

b

c

d

e

f

15 CD1 54 **Listen again and complete the sentences.**

1 Jake learned to cook when he was _____ .
2 His _____ works in a restaurant.
3 He made _____ for the competition.
4 His surprise ingredient was _____ .
5 You eat the curry with _____ .

16 CD1 55 **Plan a cooking competition with your friends.**

What would you like to cook? I'd like to cook …

Great! What do you need for … ? You need …

When do you eat it? You eat it for …

Skills: *Reading and writing*

 What does Talia like making?

17 **Read and listen.**

Sweet ambition

My name is Talia Asp, and I'm from Bergen, in Norway. I want to be a gingerbread artist when I'm older because I like art and I love cooking. Gingerbread is a type of cookie. It's good for art because you can cut it into different shapes.

I like making gingerbread houses the most. They're like a puzzle. You cut the gingerbread into pieces and bake them in the oven. Then you put the pieces together and decorate the house with candy. My mom wanted me to make this house for her birthday.

My town, Bergen, is famous for its gingerbread art. Every December, we make the biggest gingerbread town in the world. There are houses, trains, boats, and cars. This year, my class made a gingerbread boat. Come and visit someday!

18 **Read again and answer the questions.**

1 Where is Talia from?
2 Does she like cooking?
3 What kind of food is gingerbread?
4 What does Talia enjoy making the most?
5 What can you see in Bergen's gingerbread town?
6 What did Talia's class make?

Your turn!

Design some gingerbread art.
What does it look like?
How many pieces of gingerbread do you need?
Who's it for?

Now write about it in your notebook.

Why is it **important** to drink water?

44

1 CD1 57 Listen and repeat.

humans

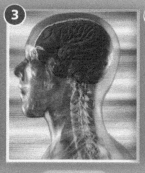
blood

brain

skin

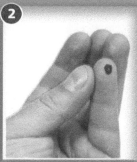
perspiration

2 Watch the video.

3 CD1 58 Read and listen.

All plants, animals, and humans need water to live. That's because our bodies need water for nearly everything they do. Our blood needs water to move around the body. Our stomachs need water to digest food. More than 70% of our brains are water, so drinking water helps us think better.

When we do sports and when it's hot, we lose water through our skin. This body water is called perspiration. We put water into our bodies when we drink and eat. When we lose more water than we put into our bodies, we feel tired and we sometimes have a headache. That's why it's important to drink 6–8 glasses of water a day.

Guess What!

Frogs don't drink. Water goes into their bodies through their skin.

Project

6 Find out how many glasses of water you and someone in your family drink each day for a week. Make a bar chart.

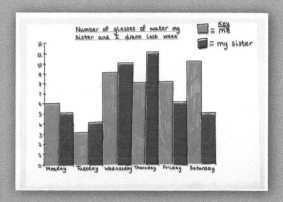

4 Answer the questions.

1 Why does our blood need water?
2 How much of our brain is water?
3 From which part of our body do we lose water when it's hot?
4 What happens when we don't drink much water?

5 When do you think you should drink more water?

→ Workbook page 36

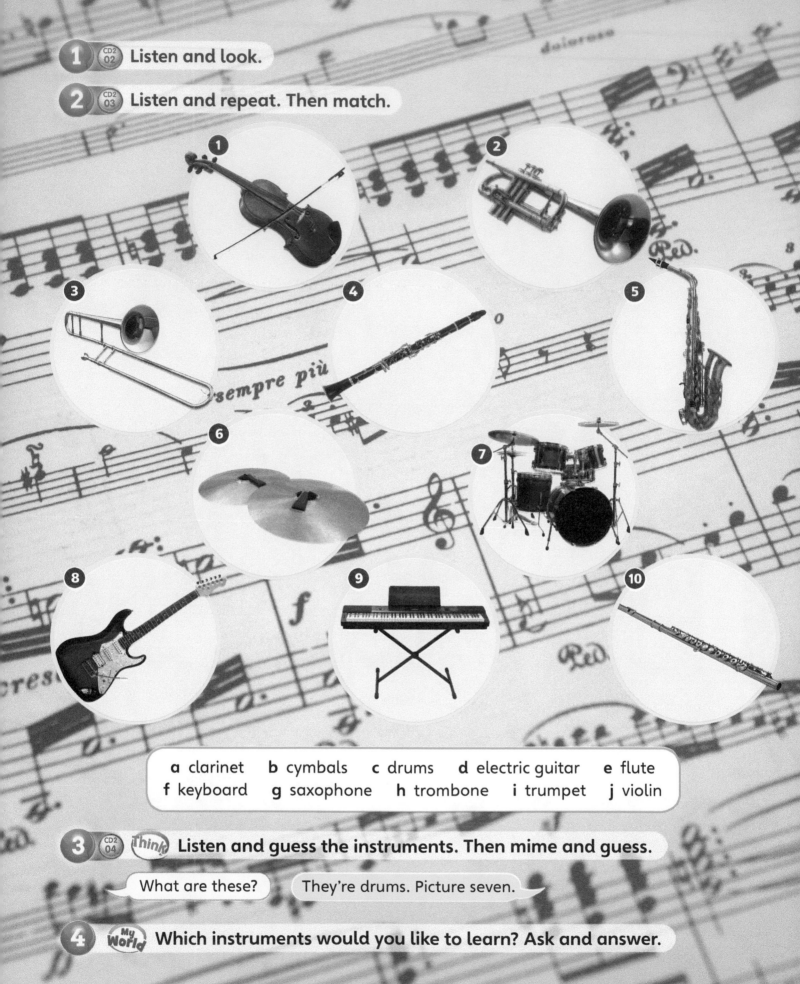

1 [CD2 02] Listen and look.

2 [CD2 03] Listen and repeat. Then match.

a clarinet   **b** cymbals   **c** drums   **d** electric guitar   **e** flute
f keyboard   **g** saxophone   **h** trombone   **i** trumpet   **j** violin

3 [CD2 04] (Think) Listen and guess the instruments. Then mime and guess.

What are these?   They're drums. Picture seven.

4 (My World) Which instruments would you like to learn? Ask and answer.

5 **Read, listen, and say the names.**

Weekends are very noisy at our house. My children all love music.

1 My oldest daughter is the best at music. She plays the guitar well, and she sings beautifully.

2 My son is learning to play the trumpet. He doesn't play badly, but he plays very slowly.

3 My youngest daughter is only three, but she likes playing the keyboard – very loudly!

Sam

Elisa

Jasmine

6 **Read and say _true_ or _false_.**

1 Jasmine plays the guitar badly.

2 Jasmine sings well.

3 Sam can't play the trumpet quickly.

4 Elisa likes playing the cymbals.

5 Elisa doesn't play the keyboard quietly.

Focus!

He plays the trumpet slowly.
She sings beautifully.
She plays the guitar well.

7 **Think** **Listen and choose the words.**

1 She's playing the violin **quickly/slowly**.

2 He's singing **well/badly**.

3 She's playing the flute **loudly/quietly**.

4 He's playing the electric guitar **loudly/quietly**.

5 She's playing the clarinet **badly/beautifully**.

Say it!

8 **Do the ends of the question and answer go up or down? Listen and repeat.**

Do you play the violin well? ↗   No, I play it badly. ↘

9 How does Emma play the electric guitar?
Listen and choose.

a badly   b loudly   c quietly

10 Listen again and practice.

Carla: Hi, Emma. What are you doing?
Emma: I'm going to band practice.
Carla: Cool! What instrument do you play?
Emma: I'm learning to play the electric guitar,
         and I sometimes sing.
Carla: Are you good at singing?
Emma: Not really. Pedro sings more beautifully than
         I do, but I play the guitar better than he does.
Carla: Who plays more loudly, you or Pedro?
Emma: I do, of course!

11   **My World** **Answer the questions with a friend. Then
         tell the class.**

> **Focus!**
>
> Pedro sings **more
> beautifully than** I do.
> I play the guitar **better
> than** he does.
> Who plays **more loudly**,
> you or Pedro? I do.

1 Who sings more
   beautifully, you or your
   friend?

2 Who plays an instrument
   better?

3 Who sings more loudly?

4 Who reads more
   quickly?

5 Who speaks more
   quietly?

6 Who eats more slowly?

7 Who laughs more
   loudly?

8 Who writes more
   beautifully?

Max sings more loudly than I do, but I sing more beautifully.

I read more slowly than Anna does.

12 **Go to page 102. Listen and repeat the chant.**

Skills: *Listening and speaking*

Let's start! What traditional instruments do you have in your country?

14 CD2 12 **Listen and match the instruments to the countries.**

1

erhu

2

vuvuzela

3

bagpipes

4

bongos

5

bouzouki

a South Africa   **b** Cuba   **c** Scotland   **d** China   **e** Greece

15 CD2 12 **Listen again and choose the words.**
1 People **sometimes/never** play the erhu in rock bands.
2 People usually play the vuvuzela **loudly/quietly**.
3 **All/Some** bouzoukis have eight strings.
4 People usually play bongos with **their hands/sticks**.
5 Bagpipes are **easy/difficult** to play.

16 CD2 13 **Talk Time** **Decide which instrument you would like to play.**

Which instrument would you like to play?   I'd like to play the …

How do you play the … ?   You play it like a …

Do you think it's easy or difficult?   I think it's …

Skills: *Reading and writing*

 Look below! **What are these instruments made from?**

17 CD2 14 **Read and listen.**

The Vegetable Orchestra

We eat vegetables every day, but what else can we do with vegetables?

In Austria, there is a vegetable orchestra. They make all their own instruments – trumpets, drums, violins, clarinets – and they make them all from vegetables.

The orchestra plays concerts all over the world. Before each concert, the musicians go to the market and buy fresh vegetables. Then they make their instruments slowly and carefully. It takes about three hours because they have to make more than forty instruments for each concert. They love inventing new instruments with different vegetables from around the world.

People always enjoy listening to the Vegetable Orchestra, and after each concert, they enjoy a bowl of vegetable soup! The orchestra's cook makes it from unused vegetables. It's delicious!

18 **Read again and correct the sentences.**
1 The Vegetable Orchestra is from Russia.
2 They make all their instruments from fruit.
3 They buy their vegetables at the supermarket.
4 The musicians make their instruments quickly.
5 They need more than twenty instruments for each concert.
6 People enjoy noodles after the concert.

Your turn!

Design an unusual instrument.
What is it made from?
What does it sound like?
How do you play it?

Now write about it in your notebook.

How do string instruments make high and low sounds?

1 (CD2 15) **Listen and repeat.**

1 vibrate

2 make tighter

3 thick string   thin string

2 **Watch the video.**

3 (CD2 16) **Read and listen.**

When we play a guitar or another string instrument, we make the strings vibrate. When a string vibrates quickly, it makes a high sound. When it vibrates slowly, it makes a low sound. The pitch is how high or low the sound is. How can we change the pitch? There are three ways.

- We can make the string tighter. Tight strings vibrate faster, so they make a higher pitch.
- We can make the string shorter because shorter strings vibrate faster, too.
- We can use thick and thin strings. Thick strings vibrate slowly and make a low sound. Thin strings vibrate quickly and make a high sound.

Guess What!

When a sound has a very high pitch, sometimes we can't hear it, but dogs can.

4 **Answer the questions.**

1 What word describes how high or low sounds are?
2 What do we hear when something vibrates slowly?
3 Which makes a higher sound, a long string or a short string?
4 Which makes a lower sound, a thick string or a thin string?

5 **What sounds do you hear every day? Do they have a high or a low pitch?**

Project

6 **Find out about an instrument. Draw it and describe how it makes sounds. How can you change the pitch?**

Ocarina

This is an ocarina. You blow into it to make a sound. The ocarina can make high sounds and low sounds. You can put your finger on the holes to change the pitch. When you put your finger on all the holes, it makes a low sound. When you don't put your finger on any holes, it makes a high sound.

Review Units 3 and 4

1 **Read, listen, and choose the words.**

I'm in the school **orchestra/band** with my friend Sally. Sally plays the **flute/drums**, and I play the **clarinet/trumpet**. My family wanted me to learn the **flute/electric guitar**, but I love playing the trumpet **loudly/quietly**!

Last year, our **band/orchestra** went to Moscow to enter a **music/cooking** competition. It was fun, but it was hard work, too. Our teacher wanted **us/me** to learn some very difficult **recipes/music**.

The competition was on the **first/last** evening of our stay. We played **badly/well**, but another **orchestra/band** played more **beautifully/quietly** than we did. **We/They** won the competition, and **we/they** came second.

After the competition, we went to a **restaurant/café** to have dinner. Sally had **fish and chips/noodles**, but I chose **curry/stew** because I wanted to try it. It was delicious!

Maria

2 **Read again and say** *true* **or** *false*.
1 Maria's family wanted her to learn the trumpet.
2 Maria enjoys playing her trumpet loudly.
3 They entered a cooking competition in Moscow.
4 Maria's orchestra came second in the competition.
5 They had dinner in a hotel.
6 Maria wanted to try dumplings.

3 **My World** **Think of a competition you entered. Ask and answer.**
What type of competition was it?
Where was it?
What did you do to prepare?
Did you win?

4 **Write about the competition in your notebook.**

5 Play the game.

Start here!

SUPERMARKET

2 tenciral

3 splugmind

4 You go to the supermarket to buy some sushi. Miss a turn.

5 lodsone

6 You ate the sushi very quickly, and you're still hungry. Go back to the supermarket.

7 bekbas

8 hoxpasneo

9 Someone is singing beautifully. Go to the café to listen. Miss a turn.

10 You stop at the market to buy an old trumpet. Miss a turn.

11 Your friends want you to try rice and beans. Go back to the café.

12 smurd

13 You can only play the old trumpet very quietly and badly. Go back to the market.

14 You go to the restaurant to have curry, and you eat very slowly. Miss a turn.

15 lambycs

16 You want your friend to practice the piano. Go back to the restaurant.

17 You don't want the other band to arrive earlier than you. Go to 18.

18 satoc

19 You don't have your electric guitar. Go back to the market to buy another one.

20 INTERNATIONAL FESTIVAL

MARKET

RESTAURANT

CAFE LIVE MUSIC

Green Find the word.

Purple Follow the instruction.

5 Now and then

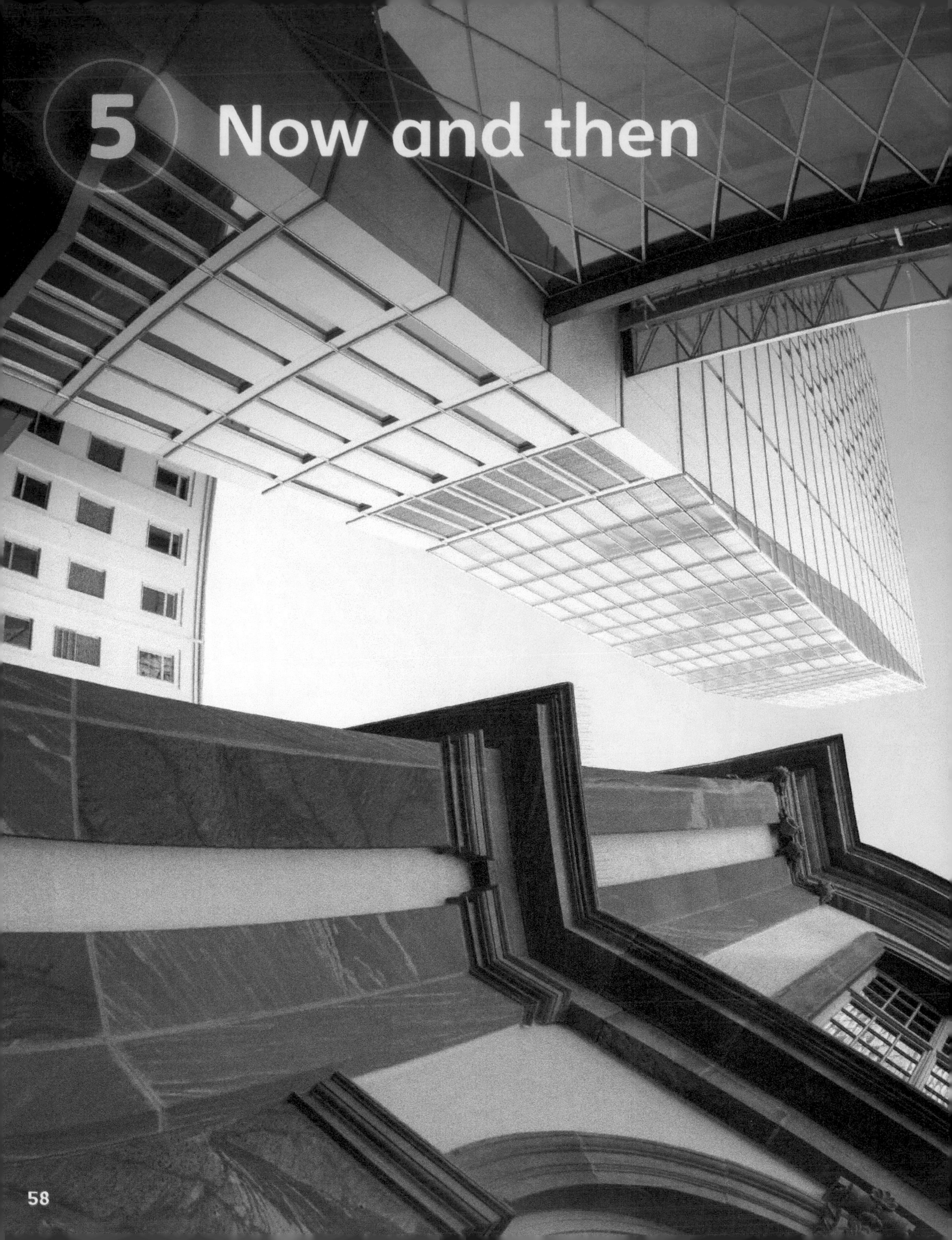

1 CD2 18 **Listen and look.**

2 CD2 19 **Listen and repeat. Then match.**

a dictionary   **b** e-book   **c** email   **d** encyclopedia   **e** letter
f magazine   **g** newspaper   **h** online game   **i** text message   **j** website

3 CD2 20 Think **Listen and guess the words. Then practice with a friend.**

You read this on an e-reader.   An e-book!

4 My World **What information technology do you use? Ask and answer.**

 **Read and listen.**

Life in 1980

Sally Rogers was born in 1980. How was life different then?

Most people didn't have a computer at home in 1980. They couldn't use the Internet or websites. They watched the news on TV or they bought newspapers, magazines, or books. They couldn't buy e-books. People could call or send letters to their friends, but they couldn't send emails. Now we can send emails to friends all over the world.

6 What could people do before 1980? Read and choose.

1 People **could/couldn't** use websites.
2 They **could/couldn't** buy books.
3 They **could/couldn't** send letters.
4 They **could/couldn't** buy encyclopedias.
5 They **could/couldn't** use the Internet.

> **Focus!**
>
> People **could buy** books in 1980. They **couldn't buy** e-books.

7 Think Read and find the mistakes in Sally's to-do list.

February 8, 1989

* Ask Dad for an e-book for my birthday.
* Send Grandma an email.
* Ask Mom to buy my favorite magazine.
* Use the Internet to do my science project.
* Check Jane's website.

> People couldn't buy e-books in 1989!

Say it!

8 Which words sound the strongest? Listen and repeat.

People could **read books**.   They **couldn't send emails**.

9 **What is Alex doing? Listen and choose.**

a watching television   b reading a book
c playing an online game

10 **Listen again and practice.**

Grandpa: What are you doing, Alex?
Alex: I'm playing online chess with Pedro.
Grandpa: Online chess?
Alex: Can you play online chess, Grandpa?
Grandpa: No, I can't. I'm not good at using computers.
Alex: Could you play online games when you were young?
Grandpa: No, I couldn't. There weren't any computers then.
Alex: Could you watch television?
Grandpa: Yes, I could. We had a television,
but it was black and white.
Alex: Could you read books?
Grandpa: Yes, of course, Alex. I'm not that old!

11 My World **Make questions. Then ask and answer.**

Focus!

Could you **play** online games
when you were young?
Yes, I **could.** / No, I **couldn't.**

play online games	use the Internet
cook	swim
read e-books	write your name
send text messages	use a dictionary
play a musical instrument	speak English

Could you use the Internet when you were 1?

No, I couldn't.

Could you swim when you were 7?

Yes, I could.

12 **Go to page 103. Listen and repeat the chant.**

Skills: *Listening and speaking*

Let's start! How do you communicate with your friends?

14 (CD2 27) **When were these forms of communication invented? Listen and match.**

a smoke signals

b the World Wide Web

c telegram

POST OFFICE TELEGRAM

d telephone

e letters

1800 BCE	600 BCE	1844	1876	1990–1991

15 (CD2 27) **Listen again and answer the questions.**

1 Which is the oldest form of communication?
2 Could people send letters in the post in 600 BCE?
3 Could people send telegrams more quickly or more slowly than letters?
4 What did Alexander Graham Bell invent?
5 Is communication easier or more difficult with the Internet?

16 (CD2 28) **(Talk Time) Talk about forms of communication with a friend.**

> Which forms of communication do you use?   I use ...

> Which do you use the most?   I use ... the most.

> What do you use it for?   I use it for ...

Skills: *Reading and writing*

 Where does Kim work?

17 **Read and listen.**

Virtual learning

Pilar is learning Chinese. But she isn't studying it at school. She has lessons with a virtual teacher at home. We asked her some questions.

Is your virtual teacher a real person?
Yes, of course. Her name is Kim, and she lives in China. She's called a virtual teacher because she teaches me online. I download activities from a website. Then I email my work to Kim, and she checks it.

Can you talk to each other?
Yes, we use a video chat tool. We have conversation classes, and I ask her questions.

Where does Kim work?
She works at home, in a café, and even on vacation! She just needs a computer and the Internet.

Do you like virtual learning?
Yes, it's fun. I live in Spain, but I have lessons in China!

18 **Read again and complete the sentences.**

1 Pilar is studying Chinese at ▭ .
2 A virtual teacher teaches ▭ .
3 Pilar downloads work from a ▭ , and ▭ it to Kim.
4 Pilar and Kim use a video chat tool to ▭ .
5 Kim uses a ▭ and the ▭ for her work.
6 Pilar thinks virtual learning is ▭ .

 Your turn!

Think about technology you have in your school.
What do you use it for?
What technology would you like to have?
Would you like to have a virtual teacher?

Now write about it in your notebook.

What do **primary sources** tell us about life in the past?

1 (CD2 30) Listen and repeat.

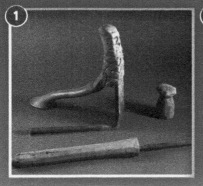
1 tools

2 statue

3 jewelry

4 board game

2 Watch the video.

3 (CD2 31) Read and listen.

A primary source is something old that tells us about life in the past. It can be an old tool, a statue, some jewelry, or a board game that people had in the past. History books that we read in school are not primary sources. This is because the writers of school books didn't live at the time they are writing about.

We can learn about the past by asking questions about primary sources. We can ask: *What did people use this tool for? Who made this statue and why did they make it? What is this jewelry made of? How did people play this board game?* When we can answer these questions, we learn about life in the past.

Guess What!

We know that the Egyptian alphabet had about 700 hieroglyphs because of primary sources.

4 Answer the questions.

1 What is a primary source?
2 What are examples of primary sources?
3 Why is a textbook about history not a primary source?
4 Why should we ask questions about primary sources?

5 What questions would you like to ask about the primary sources above?

Project

6 Find out about a primary source that tells us about life in the past. Make an information sheet about it.

An old photograph

This old photograph is a primary source. It tells us about life in the past. We can see two children playing hoops. Hoops is a very old game. Children played this game in the street. They ran with the hoops and used sticks to hit them. Some hoops were metal, and some were wood.

6 The environment

1 (CD2 32) **Listen and look.**

2 (CD2 33) **Listen and repeat. Then match.**

a aluminum **b** cardboard **c** electricity **d** gas **e** glass
f paper **g** plastic **h** solar power **i** water **j** wind power

3 (CD2 34) (Think) **Listen and say *good* or *bad for the environment*. Then practice.**

We use solar power in our house. Good for the environment.

4 (My World) **What do you do for the environment at home? Ask and answer.**

5  **Read and listen.**

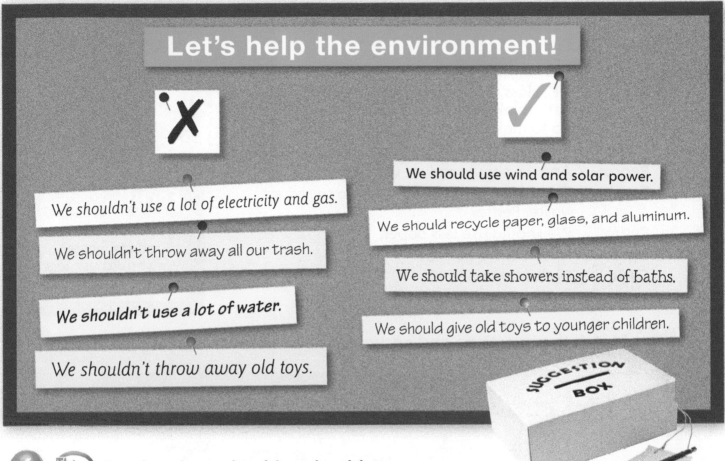

Let's help the environment!

X

We shouldn't use a lot of electricity and gas.

We shouldn't throw away all our trash.

We shouldn't use a lot of water.

We shouldn't throw away old toys.

✓

We should use wind and solar power.

We should recycle paper, glass, and aluminum.

We should take showers instead of baths.

We should give old toys to younger children.

SUGGESTION BOX

6 (Think) **Read and say *should* or *shouldn't*.**

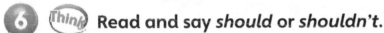

1 We _____ reuse plastic bags.
2 W e _____ use a lot of gas.
3 We _____ turn off televisions and computers at night.
4 We _____ throw away glass bottles.
5 We _____ recycle cardboard.

Focus!

We **should use** wind and solar power. We **shouldn't use** a lot of electricity.

7 (My World) **Think of more ideas to help the environment.**

We shouldn't always go to school by car.

We should walk or ride a bike.

We should make art from trash!

Say it!

8  **How do we say the green parts of these words? Listen and repeat.**

pap**er**	c**ir**cus	sol**ar**	pow**er**
wat**er**	**for**get	comput**er**	h**our**

9 What do they want to make more eco-friendly?
Listen and choose.

a Pedro's house   b Carla's house   c their school

 10 Listen again and practice.

Teacher: OK, class. It's Environment Day today.
Let's think about our school. What should we
do to make our school more eco-friendly?

Carla: We shouldn't waste energy. We should save it.

Pedro: And we should reduce waste.

Teacher: Good idea. What should we do to reduce
waste, Pedro?

Pedro: We should use less paper.

Teacher: How can we do that?

Carla: Do less homework?

Teacher: Carla!

Focus!

What **should** we **do**
to reduce waste?
We **should use** less
paper.

 11 **Match the questions and answers. Then ask and answer.**

1 _____ ?
We should use solar power in
the summer.

2 _____ ?
We should collect rainwater to
use on our yards.

3 _____ ?
We should write on both sides of
paper.

4 _____ ?
We should plant new trees.

5 _____ ?
We should recycle or reuse our
trash.

a What should we do to save forests?
b What should we do to save energy?
c What should we do to save water?
d What should we do to save paper?
e What should we do to reduce waste?

What should we do to save energy?

We should turn off the TV at night.

 12 Go to page 103. Listen and repeat the chant.

Skills: *Listening and speaking*

14 CD2 41 Which eco-home do the Smith family want to visit? Listen and say the letter.

a

b

c

d

15 CD2 41 Listen again and correct the sentences.

1 Each flat in Bosco Verticale has vegetables on its balcony.
2 The grass on the grass roof house helps keep the house warm.
3 The house on the wind farm is expensive.
4 The house with solar panels is in the city.
5 The girl thinks the house with solar panels is the most beautiful.

16 CD2 42 **Talk Time** Design an eco-friendly home with a friend.

Should we design a ... ?   OK. What energy should we use?

Let's use ...   Good idea.

What special features should we add?   Let's add ...

Skills: *Reading and writing*

 Look below! **What is this animal made from?**

17 CD1 43 **Read and listen.**

A flip-flop safari

The company Ocean Sole, in Kenya, East Africa, makes beautiful toys and sculptures of animals. They make colorful elephants, giraffes, lions, rhinos, dolphins, sharks, turtles, and a lot more.

But there's something very special about these animals. They're made from old flip-flops! Every year, people find thousands of old rubber flip-flops on the beaches in East Africa. They make the beaches and oceans dirty, and they are dangerous for fish and sea animals.

Ocean Sole workers collect the flip-flops and clean them. Then they recycle the rubber and plastic from the flip-flops and make the toys and sculptures. They sell their animals in zoos, aquariums, and stores all over the world. Ocean Sole helps clean the beaches and gives jobs to local people, too.

Would you like to go on a flip-flop safari?

18 **Read again and answer the questions.**
1 Which country is Ocean Sole from?
2 What do they make sculptures of?
3 What do they use to make their sculptures?
4 Why are flip-flops a problem for the beaches?
5 What does Ocean Sole do with the flip-flops before they make sculptures?
6 What do they do with the sculptures?

Your turn!

Design a piece of recycled art.
What is it made from?
What does it look like?
Is it a sculpture or a toy?

Now write about it in your notebook.

What happens to our old glass bottles?

1 CD2 44 Listen and repeat.

machine

sand

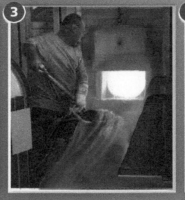
furnace

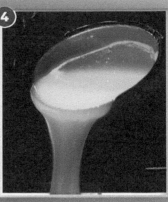
melt

2 Watch the video.

3 CD2 45 Read and listen.

When we finish using our glass bottles, we put them in a recycling bin. A big truck takes the bottles to a recycling center. The people at the recycling center sort the glass by color.

A big machine breaks the glass into small pieces. Another machine mixes the pieces of glass with sand. They put the glass and sand in a special oven called a "furnace". The furnace is very hot. The mixed glass and sand melt and become liquid. When the glass is liquid, they can change its shape to make new bottles.

They send the new bottles to factories so they can use them again. Recycling glass uses less energy than making new glass, so it's better for the environment.

Guess What!

Recycling one glass bottle saves enough energy to power a TV for 20 minutes.

Project

6 Find out about how people recycle paper, plastic, or aluminum. Make a flow chart.

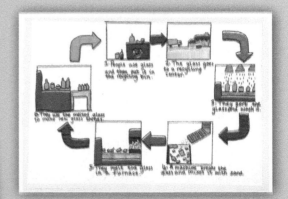

4 Answer the questions.

1 Where should we put our old glass bottles?
2 What do they mix the pieces of glass with?
3 Why does the glass melt?
4 Why is recycling glass good for the environment?

5 Which objects would you like to make from recycled glass?

Review Units 5 and 6

1 **Read, listen, and choose the words.**

Last spring, there was a bad storm near my town.
We didn't have any **electricity/gas** for a week.
We had **wind power/gas** and **water/paper**,
but things were difficult without **gas/electricity**.

Mom **could/couldn't** work because she
could/couldn't use her computer or send
emails/letters. I was bored because I
couldn't/shouldn't watch television or
play **chess/online games** with my friends, and
I **could/couldn't** do my homework. I needed to
use **the Internet/a website** because I had to
do a project on **communication/aluminum**. Mom
said I **should/shouldn't** use an **encyclopedia/dictionary**
for my project. I finished that quickly, but I was still bored!
So I visited my friend, and we read an interesting **magazine/newspaper**.
We read about a new **plastic/solar** laptop. It doesn't need
gas/electricity because it uses **solar/wind** power.
I told Mom we **should/shouldn't** buy one!

Oscar

2 **Read again and answer the questions.**
1 Why didn't Oscar have any electricity?
2 Why couldn't his mother work?
3 What couldn't Oscar do without electricity?
4 What did he use to do his homework?
5 What did he do with his friend?
6 What does Oscar want to buy?

3 **My World** **Imagine you had no electricity last week. Ask and answer.**
What couldn't you do?   What did you do instead?   How did you feel?

4 **Write about what you did without electricity in your notebook.**

→ Workbook pages 64–65

5 Play the game.

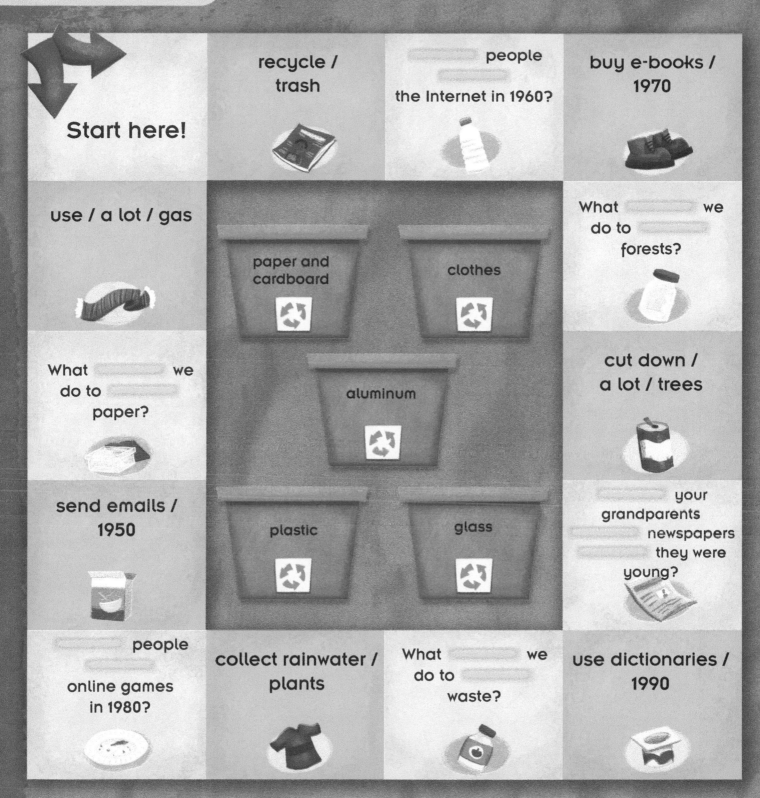

Start here!

recycle / trash

people the Internet in 1960?

buy e-books / 1970

use / a lot / gas

paper and cardboard

clothes

What _____ we do to forests?

What _____ we do to paper?

aluminum

cut down / a lot / trees

send emails / 1950

plastic

glass

_____ your grandparents _____ newspapers they were young?

_____ people online games in 1980?

collect rainwater / plants

What _____ we do to waste?

use dictionaries / 1990

Yellow
Complete the questions and answer them.

Blue
Make true sentences using these words.

7 Space

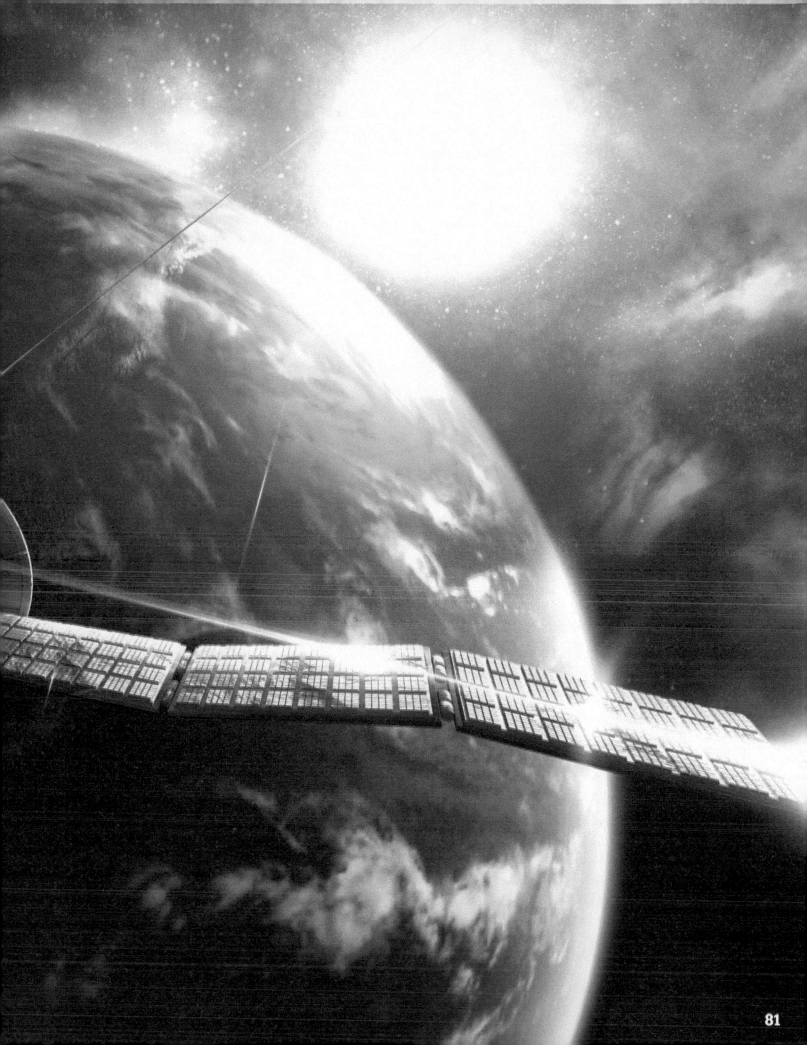

1 (CD3 02) **Listen and look.**

2 (CD3 03) **Listen and repeat. Then match.**

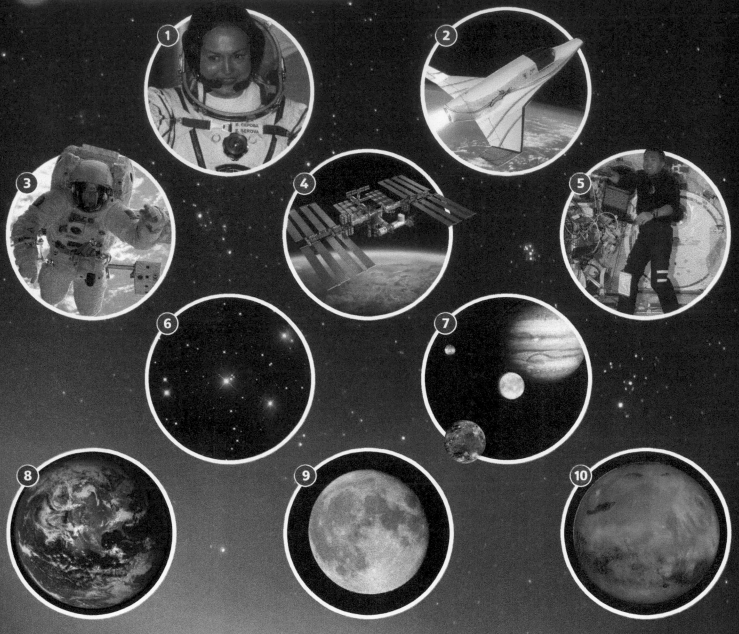

a astronaut   **b** Earth   **c** Mars   **d** planets   **e** space laboratory
f space station   **g** spacecraft   **h** spacesuit   **i** stars   **j** the Moon

3 (CD3 04) **Think** **Listen and guess the words. Then practice with a friend.**

These are big, round things in space. They move around the Sun.   Planets!

4 **My World** **Would you like to be an astronaut? Ask and answer.**

5 **Read and listen.**

The astronauts in this spacecraft are ready for their next mission. They're going to travel to the International Space Station. They're going to live and work on the space station for six months. They aren't going to see their families for a long time!

They're going to work in a space laboratory.

They're going to fix the outside of the space station.

They're going to eat space food.

They're going to look at Earth from space.

6 **Read and say *true* or *false*.**

1 The astronauts are going to visit Mars.
2 They're going to live in the space station for half a year.
3 They aren't going to work outside.
4 They aren't going to eat normal food.
5 They are going to see our planet.

Focus!

They're going to travel.
They aren't going to see their families.

7 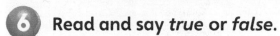 **Make sentences about a friend. Then check.**

when you're older   next weekend   after school   for your birthday

You're going to be an astronaut when you're older.

No, I'm not. I'm going to be a doctor.

You're going to play soccer after school.

Yes, I am. You're right!

Say it!

8 **How do we say *going to* in these sentences? Listen and repeat.**

They're going to go into space.   They aren't going to see the Moon.

What are they talking about? Listen and choose.

  a a space camp   **b** space travel   **c** a space station

 Listen again and practice.

Emma: I'm going to go to a space camp next week. I'm going to stay for five nights.

Alex: Space camp?! What are you going to do there?

Emma: We're going to learn about space missions.

Alex: Are you going to travel in a spacecraft?

Emma: No, we aren't. Don't be silly. But we *are* going to fly a spacecraft in the simulator, and we're going to explore a real spacecraft.

Alex: Are you going to meet astronauts?

Emma: Yes, we are.

Alex: Wow! Can I come, too?

Focus!

What **are** you **going to** do?
Are you **going to** travel in a spacecraft?
Yes, we **are**. / No, we **aren't**.

 Imagine you're at space camp. Choose three activities you're going to do and compare with your friends.

SPACE CAMP

Explore a real spacecraft.
Build a model spacecraft.
Climb the Mars climbing wall.
Sit on a zero gravity chair.
Learn about the history of space travel.
Eat space food.
Go on a moon walk.
Wear a real spacesuit.
Watch Earth from space in a 3-D movie.
Fly a spacecraft in the simulator.
Meet astronauts.

What are you going to do at space camp?   I'm going to climb the Mars climbing wall.

Are you going to eat space food?   No, I'm not. I'm going to go on a moon walk.

 Go to page 103. Listen and repeat the chant.

2 Find the brightest star you can see. Under this star there's a tree. Look under the tree for your final clue. It's something round and blue.

1 I don't understand. The map says Emoclew is here.

Yes, but Emoclew is a lost city, remember?

3 OK. Where's the brightest star?

There!

4 So that's the tree. Come on!

5 We need to look under it.

6 Wow!

It's a wheel!

7 Guess the password and all of you can enter the city of Emoclew.

8 What's the password, Sofia?

I don't know. My game wasn't finished, remember?

9 Let's guess. There are seven letters.

It starts with W.

Skills: *Listening and speaking*

Let's start! What training do you think astronauts need?

14 What training do astronauts need? Listen and say the letters.

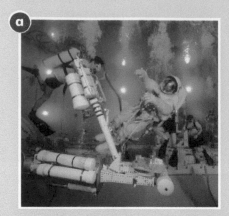

a

b

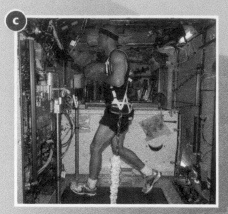

c

d

e

15 (CD3 11) **Listen again and choose the words.**

1 All astronauts have to speak **Russian/English**.
2 Astronauts learn to fly a spacecraft to the **International Space Station/Moon**.
3 Astronauts practice floating in zero gravity in **aircraft/spacecraft**.
4 Astronauts practice space walks **underwater/in a simulator**.
5 Astronauts have to exercise every **day/week**.

16 (CD3 12) **Talk about space travel with a friend.**

How do you feel about space travel?   I think it's …

Would you like to travel to … ?   Yes, I would. / No, I wouldn't.

What would you like to do in space?   I'd like to …

Skills: *Reading and writing*

 Look below! **What is this robot doing?**

 17 **Read and listen.**

Is life possible on Mars?

Pictures from space show that Mars is a cold, dry, and rocky planet. Scientists at NASA want to discover if life is or was possible on Mars. They're searching for water and signs of life. But they aren't sending astronauts to Mars. They're using robots.

The *Curiosity* rover landed on Mars on August 6, 2012. It's a robotic laboratory. The rover has seventeen special cameras and lots of other tools. It explores Mars, and it collects rock and soil samples. It can break rocks with a laser, and it collects samples with a special arm. Then it uses computers to study the samples, and it sends information back to Earth.

From this information, scientists know there was once water on Mars. Do you think the rover is going to find signs of life?

18 **Read again and answer the questions.**

1 What is the planet Mars like?
2 What are scientists looking for on Mars?
3 When did the *Curiosity* rover land on Mars?
4 What does it collect and study?
5 What does it use computers for?
6 What do scientists now know about Mars?

Your turn!

Design a space robot.
What is it going to look like?
Which planet is it going to explore?
What is it going to find out?

Now write about it in your notebook.

How are the
planets different?

1 🔊 CD3 14 Listen and repeat.

solar system

orbit

reflect

2 Watch the video.

3 🔊 CD3 15 Read and listen.

The eight planets in our solar system all orbit the Sun, but they're not all the same. The four planets closest to the Sun are made of rock and metal. The other planets are made of gas. The smallest planet is Mercury, and the biggest planet is Jupiter. Jupiter is bigger than all of the other planets put together!

When we look at the night sky, Venus is brighter than the other planets. This is because its thick clouds reflect the light from the Sun and because it's the closest planet to Earth.

Some planets have a moon. Moons orbit their planet. Some planets have more than one moon. Jupiter has 63 moons! How many moons does Earth have?

Guess What!

Mercury is the closest planet to the Sun, but Venus is the hottest.

4 Answer the questions.

1 What do the planets move around in space?
2 Which planet is bigger, Earth or Mercury?
3 Look at the picture on page 88. Which planet is Jupiter?
4 Do all the planets have a moon?

5 Which planet would you like to learn more about?

Project

6 Find out about a planet in our solar system. Write a factfile about it.

Planet name: Venus
Size: about the same as Earth
Position from the Sun: 2nd planet from the Sun
Orbit around the Sun: 225 days
Fun fact: Venus is the hottest planet in our solar system

Celebrations

1 (CD3 16) **Listen and look.**

2 (CD3 17) **Listen and repeat. Then match.**

a clown   **b** costume   **c** dancer   **d** dragon   **e** fireworks
f float   **g** amusement park   **h** mask   **i** musician   **j** pirate

3 (CD3 18) **Think** **Listen and say _yes_ or _no_. Then ask and answer.**

Does a musician play an instrument?   Yes!

4 **My World** **What's your favorite celebration? Ask and answer.**

5 (CD3 19) **Read and listen.**

My town carnival

Focus!

The town **where** we had our parade.
The costume **that** I made.
My friend **who** lives on my street.

1

This is the town where
we had our parade.

2

This is me in the
costume that I made.

3

This is my friend who
lives on my street.

4

These are my cousins who
gave us some candy.

6 **Read and match to make sentences about the photographs.**
Then say the photograph number.

1 It's a girl …
2 It's a drum …
3 They're people …
4 It's a street …

a that a boy played in the carnival.
b where they watched the parade.
c who dressed up as a clown.
d who danced in the parade.

It's a girl who dressed up as a clown.   Photograph two.

7 (World) **Choose and make sentences. Then ask a friend to guess.**

a friend who   a place where   a thing that

He's a friend who has a big dog.   Miguel!

It's a thing that we use to write.   A pen!

8 (CD3 20) **Go to page 103. Listen and repeat the chant.**

9 (CD3 21) **Where did Alex have his birthday?**
Listen and choose.

a Italy b the United Kingdom c Spain

10 (CD3 21) **Listen again and practice.**

Carla: What did you do for your birthday, Alex?
Alex: I visited my friend Luis.
Carla: Luis? Is that your friend who lives in Spain?
Alex: Yes. I went to Madrid, and we went to an amusement park. I took some great photographs – look!
Carla: Wow! That ride looks scary!
Alex: Yes, it went really high, but it was great.
Carla: Is this the place where you had your party?
Alex: No, Carla. That's the Royal Palace!

Focus!

Is that your friend **who** lives in Spain?
Is this the place **where** you had your party?

11 (Think) **Read about Carla's birthday party and say the missing words. Then choose a photograph and ask and answer.**

The place _____ I had my party.

The cake _____ we ate at my party.

My friend _____ dressed up as a pirate.

The clown _____ told us some jokes.

The present _____ my best friend gave me.

The yard _____ we played some games.

Is it a place?   Yes, it is.

Is it the place where she had her party?   No, it isn't.

Say it!

12 (CD3 22) (CD3 23) **Which words sound the strongest? Do the ends of the question and answer go up or down? Listen and repeat.**

Is **this** your **friend** who **lives** in **Spain**? ↗   **No**, it's my **cousin**. ↘

13 CD3 24 **Read and listen.**

1 I know! It's *Welcome*! *Emoclew* backwards!

Good job, Ruby.

2 Wow!

It's a yeti city!

3 They're happy to see our yeti!

Look! They're going to have a party.

4 EMOH OG

Wait! Emoh Og!

It's the street name that's on the envelope.

5 Here we are, number 3.

The door is open!

6 We're back in the den!

Look! I still have the letter.

7 Welcome home all of you. Thank you for finding Emoclew. The game is finished. Now your mission is to enter the competition!

8 Look at your game, Sofia. It's finished.

Game finished

You can enter the competition.

We can enter. It's our game now.

9 COMPUTER GAME COMPETITION

Good job, Sofia. Your game was the best.

This is for my friends, too. They helped me win.

→ Workbook page 77

Value: Share success with your friends

95

Skills: *Listening and speaking*

 Let's start! Do you like watching dance shows or plays? Why or why not?

 Which child is Sonia? Listen and say the letter.

 Listen and say *true* or *false*.

1 Sonia's club is going to sing in a competition.
2 They're going to dance the story of *Alice in Wonderland*.
3 There are five children who are going to play Alice.
4 Sonia made her costume.
5 Sonia's going to be the character who's wearing a big hat.

  Choose a story to act out with your friends.

What story should we act out?   Let's act out the story of …

OK. I'll be … Who do you want to be?   I'll be …

Great! Should we make … ?   Yes, and let's make …

Skills: *Reading and writing*

 Look below! **What is this float made from?**

 17 **Read and listen.**

Fantastic floats

The Flower Parade in Zundert, the Netherlands, takes place in September. It's famous for its floats, which are made of flowers. You can see fantastic animals, people, buildings, motorcycles, and even astronauts. Who makes these works of art?

Every year, there is a float competition at the parade. Twenty villages enter the competition, and each village makes one float. Most people in the village help make their float. The younger people build it out of wire, papier-mâché, and cardboard, and the older people grow thousands of flowers for it. They all work on the float for three months during the summer. Then, three days before the parade, everyone decorates the float with the flowers.

It's hard work, but the people from the village enjoy working together. They make friends and have fun, and sometimes their float wins the competition!

18 **Read again and correct the sentences.**

1 You can see the Flower Parade in October.
2 The costumes are made of flowers.
3 Thirty villages enter a float competition.
4 The younger people grow the flowers.
5 Each float needs hundreds of flowers.
6 The people from the village don't like working on their float.

Your turn!

Design a float.
What is it going to look like?
What are you going to make it from?
Which celebration is it for?

Now write about it in your notebook.

→ Workbook page 79

How do **fireworks** work?

1 🔊 CD3 28 Listen and repeat.

1 gunpowder

2 fuse

3 explode

4 metal salt

2 Watch the video.

3 🔊 CD3 29 Read and listen.

Fireworks have gunpowder inside them, and they also have a fuse. When someone lights the fuse of a firework, gas from the gunpowder pushes the firework up into the air. When the firework is in the air, the gunpowder explodes and usually makes a loud sound.

Fireworks have metal salts inside them, too. The metal salts explode with the gunpowder. Different types of metal salts make different colors when they burn. Lithium makes a red light, copper makes a green light, and sodium makes a yellow light. Some fireworks have many different metal salts, so they make lots of different colors when the gunpowder explodes.

Guess What!

Fireworks were invented more than 2,000 years ago in China.

4 Answer the questions.

1 What's inside fireworks?
2 What happens when someone lights the fuse of a firework?
3 What makes the beautiful colors in fireworks?
4 Why do some fireworks make many different colors?

5 When was the last time you saw fireworks? What were they like?

Project

6 Find out about your favorite kind of fireworks. Draw a diagram and explain how it works.

Fountain firework

paper
fuse
gunpowder and small pieces of metal
cardboard tube

1. Someone lights the fuse.
2. The gunpowder burns and makes gas.
3. The pieces of metal go up and make a fountain of colorful lights.

→ Workbook page 80

Review Units 7 and 8

1 **Read, listen, and choose the words.**

My name is Lucia, and I like **writing stories/making costumes** and drawing **pictures/masks**. Someday, I'm going to be a writer **who/which** writes books for children. At the moment, I'm writing a story about a **dragon/astronaut**. Her name's Daisy, and she's a space **pirate/clown**.

Daisy travels to **the Moon/Mars** to look for treasure, but she doesn't travel in a **plane/spacecraft**. She flies into space in a special **spacesuit/planet**.

Daisy has a map **who/that** shows that the treasure is in a cave on **the Moon/Mars**, but she doesn't find any treasure. She finds an underground city **which/where** there are lots of friendly Moon **dragons/pirates**. They're building a **float/laboratory** for their **Moon Parade/space station**, and they ask Daisy to help them.

My story isn't finished, but at the end, I think Daisy **is/isn't** going to stay on **the Moon/Mars**. She's going to decide that new friends **are/aren't** more important than treasure!

2 **Read again and match.**

1 Lucia's story is about a dragon ...
2 Daisy wants to find ...
3 Daisy thinks the treasure ...
4 Daisy makes friends with ...
5 Daisy helps the Moon dragons ...
6 Daisy is going to stay ...

a is in a Moon cave.
b who's called Daisy.
c with her new friends.
d some Moon dragons.
e treasure on the Moon.
f build a float.

3 **Think of a story character. Ask and answer.**

What's his or her name?   What's he or she like?   What's he or she going to do?

4 **Write about your story character in your notebook.**

→ Workbook pages 82–83

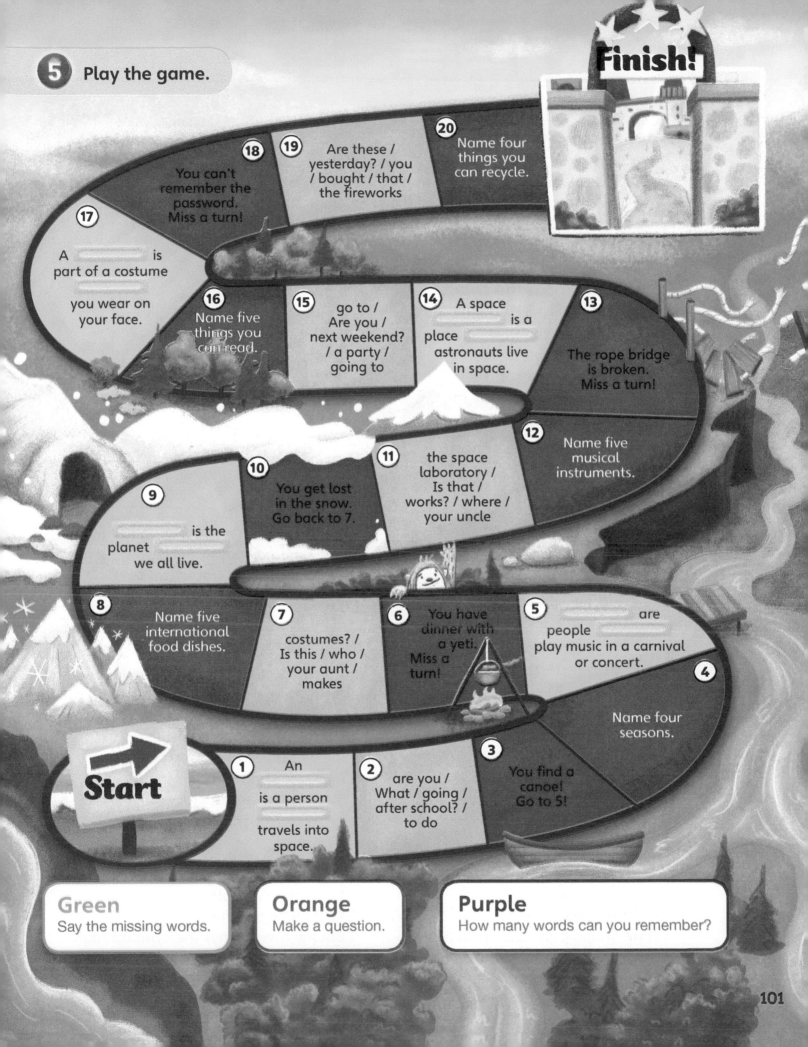

5 Play the game.

Finish!

17 A _____ is part of a costume you wear on your face.

18 You can't remember the password. Miss a turn!

19 Are these / yesterday? / you / bought / that / the fireworks

20 Name four things you can recycle.

16 Name five things you can read.

15 go to / Are you / next weekend? / a party / going to

14 A space _____ is a place astronauts live in space.

13 The rope bridge is broken. Miss a turn!

12 Name five musical instruments.

11 the space laboratory / Is that / works? / where / your uncle

10 You get lost in the snow. Go back to 7.

9 _____ is the planet we all live.

8 Name five international food dishes.

7 costumes? / Is this / who / your aunt / makes

6 You have dinner with a yeti. Miss a turn!

5 _____ are people play music in a carnival or concert.

4 Name four seasons.

Start

1 An _____ is a person travels into space.

2 are you / What / going / after school? / to do

3 You find a canoe! Go to 5!

Green
Say the missing words.

Orange
Make a question.

Purple
How many words can you remember?

101

Chants

Welcome (page 8)

 Listen and repeat the chant.

When I was five, I went to school.
Yes, I went to school when I was five.
When I went to school, I met my best friend,
And she's still my best friend now.

When I was ten, my friend moved.
Yes, she moved when I was ten.
When she moved, we both felt sad.
But we're still best friends now.

Unit 1 (page 18)

 Listen and repeat the chant.

Can you look for the flashlight, please?
Can you look for the flashlight?
What did he ask you to do?
He asked me to look for the flashlight!

Can you put up the tent, please?
Can you put up the tent?
What did he ask you to do?
He asked me to put up the tent!

Unit 2 (page 28)

 Listen and repeat the chant.

Who's better at juggling, you
or your friend?
I'm better at juggling.
I'm better than my friend.
Who's the best at cooking in your family?
My dad's the best at cooking.
He's the best in the family.

Who's worse at singing, you
or your friend?
I'm worse at singing.
I'm worse than my friend.
Who's the worst at swimming in your family?
My brother's the worst at swimming.
He's the worst in the family.

Unit 3 (page 39)

 Listen and repeat the chant.

What do you want me to do?
I want you to make some stew.
What does he want you to do?
He wants me to make some stew.
What did he want her to do?
He wanted her to make some stew!

What do you want me to do?
I want you to pick up my shoe.
What does she want you to do?
She wants me to pick up her shoe.
What did she want him to do?
She wanted him to pick up her shoe!

Unit 4 (page 50)

12 **Listen and repeat the chant.**

I play the violin well,
And I sing beautifully,
But my friend plays the violin better
than me,
And she sings more beautifully, too.

I play the cymbals loudly,
And I play the trumpet well,
But my friend plays the cymbals more
loudly than me,
And he plays the trumpet better, too.

Unit 5 (page 62)

 Listen and repeat the chant.

Could you send emails when you were young?
No, I couldn't. No, I couldn't.
I couldn't send emails when I was young.
We didn't have a computer.

Could you read books when you were young?
Yes, I could. Yes, I could.
I could read books when I was young.
I had a lot of books!

Unit 6 (page 72)

 Listen and repeat the chant.

What should we do to help our school
For Environment Day, for Environment Day?
We should save energy and reduce waste
For Environment Day, for Environment Day!

What should we do to reduce waste
For Environment Day, for Environment Day?
We should recycle trash and use less paper
For Environment Day, for Environment Day!

Unit 7 (page 84)

 Listen and repeat the chant.

Where are you going to go this weekend?
I'm going to go to a space camp.
What are you going to do there?
I'm going to eat space food.
Are you going to eat fish and chips?
No, I'm not.
I'm going to eat space food.

What are you going to do after school?
I'm going to visit my friends.
What are you going to do with them?
We're going to go to the movie theater.
Are you going to watch a movie?
Yes, we are.
We're going to go to the movie theater.

Unit 8 (page 93)

 Listen and repeat the chant.

This is the party that we had in our town.
This is my brother who dressed up as a clown.
These are the fireworks that made pretty lights.
This is the hall where we danced all night.

These are the friends who I met yesterday.
This is the fair where we stayed all day.
This is the ride that flew up in the air.
And this is the prize that I won at the fair.

Thanks and Acknowledgments

Many thanks to everyone in the excellent team at Cambridge University Press. In particular we would like to thank Emily Hird, Liane Grainger, and Melissa Bryant whose professionalism, enthusiasm, experience, and talent makes them all such a pleasure to work with.

We would also like to give special thanks to Lesley Koustaff for her unfailing support, expert guidance, good humor, and welcome encouragement throughout the project.

The authors and publishers would like to thank the following contributors:

Blooberry Design: concept design, cover design, book design, page makeup

Charlotte Aldis: editorial training

Ann Thomson: art direction

Gareth Boden Photography: commissioned photography

Alison Wright: picture research

Ian Harker: audio recording

Lisa Hutchins: freelance editing

Robert Lee, Dib Dib Dub Studios: chant composition

James Richardson: arrangement of theme tune

Vince Cross: theme tune composition

Phaebus: video production

John Marshall Media: audio recording and production

hyphen S.A.: publishing management, American English edition

The authors and publishers acknowledge the following sources of copyright material and are grateful for the permissions granted. Although every effort has been made, it has not always been possible to identify the sources of all the material used, or to trace all copyright holders. If any omissions are brought to our notice, we will be happy to include the appropriate acknowledgments on reprinting.

The authors and publishers would like to thank the following illustrators:

Pablo Gallego (Beehive Illustration): pp. 9, 19, 29, 41, 51, 63, 73, 85, 95; Mark Duffin p. 32; Marcus Cutler (Sylvie Poggio Artists): pp. 35, 57, 79, 101; Bob Lea: p. 89.

The authors and publishers would like to thank the following for permission to reproduce photographs:

Chants spread b/g: Shutterstock; Contents (b/g): Ratikova/Shutterstock; p. 4–5: Tim Gainey/Alamy; p. 6 (b/g): suns07butterfl y/Shutterstock; p. 6 (1): Peter Wey/Shutterstock; p. 6 (2): Max Sudakov/Shutterstock; p. 6 (3): scubaluna/Shutterstock; p. 6 (4): Botond Horvath/Shutterstock; p. 6 (5): Tim Gainey/Alamy; p. 6 (6): Education Images/UIG/Getty; p. 6 (7): Weeraphon Suriwongsa/Shutterstock; p. 6 (8): Pictureguy/Shutterstock; p. 6 (9): Mihai Simonia/Shutterstock; p. 7 (a): Majority World/REX Shutterstock/Rex Features; p. 7 (b): Diane Levit/Corbis; p. 7 (c): epa european pressphoto agency b.v./Alamy; p. 8 (B): Stuart Pearce/Alamy; p. 10–11 b/g: drferry/Getty; p. 10 (TL): Owe Andersson/Alamy; p. 10 (TR): Don Mason/Corbis; p. 10 (BL): Tim Gainey/Alamy; p. 10 (BR): Fotografi e Luise Boettcher/Getty; p. 11: Nicole Sharp/Shutterstock; p. 12–13 (b/g): Farianna/Shutterstock; p. 13 (1): SPPhoto/Shutterstock; p. 14–15: Mister Jo/Getty; p. 16 (b/g): Elenamiv/Shutterstock; p. 16 (1): trekandshoot/Shutterstock; p. 16 (2): Sergiy Zavgorodny/Shutterstock; p. 16 (3): Richard Peterson/Shutterstock; p. 16 (4): zirconicusso/Shutterstock; p. 16 (5): Everything/Shutterstock; p. 16 (6): Coprid/Shutterstock; p. 16 (7): Africa Studio/Shutterstock; p. 16 (8): Tyler Olson/Shutterstock; p. 16 (9): studiomode/Shutterstock; p. 16 (10): Chris Turner/Shutterstock; p. 18 (B): Hurst Photo/Shutterstock; p. 20–21 (b/g): WorldFoto/Alamy; p. 20 (a): Imagestate Media Partners Limited – Impact Photos/Alamy; p. 20 (b): fStop Images GmbH/Alamy; p. 20 (c): Aurora Photos/Alamy; p. 22–23: Stefan Mokrzecki/Getty; p. 24–25: VALENTINA PETROVA/Getty; p. 26 (b/g): LeksusTuss/Shutterstock; p. 26 (1): Andrew Paterson/Alamy; p. 26 (2): Klaus Tiedge/Corbis; p. 26 (3): wavebreakmedia/Shutterstock; p. 26 (4): alexkatkov/Shutterstock; p. 26 (5): Tatyana Vyc/Shutterstock; p. 26 (6): Stephen Coburn/Shutterstock; p. 26 (7): Anneka/Shutterstock; p. 26 (8): Blend Images/Alamy; p. 26 (10): Artamonov Yury/Shutterstock; p. 27 (BL): Brad Wynnyk/Alamy; p. 27 (BML): Glenda/Shutterstock; p. 27 (BMR): MAHATHIR MOHD YASIN/Shutterstock; p. 27 (BR): MANDY GODBEHEAR/Shutterstock; p. 28 (B): Denise Crew/Getty; p. 30–31 (b/g): Marin Tomas/Getty; p. 30 (a): Jan Sandvik Editorial/Alamy; p. 30 (b): Sheldon Levis/Alamy; p. 30 (c): David Reed/Alamy; p. 30 (d): Scott Hortop Travel/Alamy; p. 30 (e): Michael Kemp/Alamy; p. 31: Hill Street Studios/Corbis; p. 32: Sportstock/Shutterstock; p. 33 (1): Yon Marsh/Alamy; p. 33 (2): PCN Photography/Alamy; p. 33 (3): dotshock/Shutterstock; p. 33 (4): Maridav/Shutterstock; p. 34: Aaron M. Cohen/

Corbis; p. 36–37: hxdyl/Getty; p. 38 (b/g): maodoltee/Shutterstock; p. 38 (1): bundit jonwises/Shutterstock; p. 38 (fl ag 1): Joop Hoek/Shutterstock; p. 38 (2): efesan/Alamy; p. 38 (fl ag 2): Joop Hoek/Shutterstock; p. 38 (3): MaraZe/Shutterstock; p. 38 (fl ag 3): Joop Hoek/Shutterstock; p. 38 (4): Venus Angel/Shutterstock; p. 38 (fl ag 4): Joop Hoek/Shutterstock; p. 38 (5): Natalia Mylova/Shutterstock; p. 38 (fl ag 5): Joop Hoek/Shutterstock; p. 38 (6): Shutterstock; p. 38 (fl ag 6): Joop Hoek/Shutterstock; p. 38 (7): JIANG HONGYAN/Shutterstock; p. 38 (fl ag 7): zzns/Shutterstock; p. 38 (8): bonchan/Shutterstock; p. 38 (fl ag 8): Joop Hoek/Shutterstock; p. 38 (9): Janet Faye Hastings/Shutterstock; p. 38 (fl ag 9): Joop Hoek/Shutterstock; p. 30 (10): Rafaela Delli Paoli/Alamy; p. 38 (fl ag 10): Joop Hoek/Shutterstock; p. 39 (T): MITO images/Alamy; p. 40 (B): Chris Stein/Getty; p. 42–43 (b/g): MARIT HOMMEDAL/Getty; p. 43: sianc/Shutterstock; p. 44: Westend61 GmbH/Alamy; p. 45 (1): Vitalinka/Shutterstock; p. 45 (2): Dmitry Lobanov/Shutterstock; p. 45 (3): ap_i/Shutterstock; p. 45 (4): Ethan Vasquez/Alamy; p. 45 (5): epa european pressphoto agency b.v./Alamy; p. 46–47: maxoidos/Getty; p. 48 (b/g): Robynrg/Shutterstock; p. 48 (1): Vereshchagin Dmitry/Shutterstock; p. 48 (2): MIGUEL GARCIA SAAVEDRA/Shutterstock; p. 48 (3): ayzek/Shutterstock; p. 48 (4): Venus Angel/Shutterstock; p. 48 (5): OZaiachin/Shutterstock; p. 48 (6): Computer Earth/Shutterstock; p. 48 (7): Dario Sabljak/Shutterstock; p. 48 (8): Mircea Pavel/Shutterstock; p. 48 (9): nikkytok/Shutterstock; p. 48 (10): pbombaert/Shutterstock; p. 49 (L): Ben Molyneux People/Alamy; p. 49 (M): Svyatoslava Vladzimirska/Shutterstock; p. 49 (R): Zina Seletskaya/Shutterstock; p. 50 (B): DNF Style/Shutterstock; p. 52–53 (b/g): wildpixel/Getty; p. 52 (1): gkphotography/Alamy; p. 52 (2): Greatstock Photographic Library/Alamy; p. 52 (3): Universal Images Group Limited/Alamy; p. 52 (4): Ira Berger/Alamy; p. 52 (5): Vespasian/Alamy; p. 53: DAVID BEBBER/Corbis; p. 54: Bradley Wells/Getty; p. 56: Monkey Business Images/Shutterstock; p. 58–59: arturbo/Getty; p. 60 (1): amana images inc./Alamy; p. 60 (2): Giakita/Shutterstock; p. 60 (3): Art Directors & TRIP/Alamy; p. 60 (5): Jose Luis Pelaez Inc/Getty; p. 60 (6): Radius Images/Alamy; p. 60 (7): Kevin Britland/Alamy; p. 60 (8): Elly Godfroy/Alamy; p. 60 (9): Denys Prykhodov/Shutterstock; p. 60 (10): TunaStyle/Alamy; p. 61: Daily Mail/REX Shutterstock/Rex Features; p. 62 (B): Cultura Creative (RF)/Alamy; p. 64–65 (b/g): Lane Oatey/Getty; p. 64 (a): Lanmas/Alamy; p. 64 (b): CERN/Science and Society Picture Library; p. 64 (c): Linda Steward/Getty; p. 64 (d): The Protected Art Archive/Alamy; p. 64 (e): Alfi o Scisetti/Alamy; p. 65: Rob Marmion/Shutterstock; p. 66: Tuul / hemis.fr/Getty; p. 67 (1): The Art Archive/Alamy; p. 67 (2): DEA / A. JEMOLO/Getty; p. 67 (3): Getty; p. 67 (4): age footstock/Alamy; p. 67 (BR): Shutterstock; p. 68–69: Arpad Benedek/Getty; p. 70 (b/g): Zoonar/P.Jilek/Getty; p. 70 (1): majeczka/Shutterstock; p. 70 (2): Smileus/Shutterstock; p. 70 (3): ppart/Shutterstock; p. 70 (4): misima/Shutterstock; p. 70 (5): Ari N/Shutterstock; p. 70 (6): Zerbor/Shutterstock; p. 70 (7): andersphoto/Shutterstock; p. 70 (8): marco varrone/Alamy; p. 70 (9): pryzmat/Shutterstock; p. 70 (10): chaoss/Shutterstock; p. 71: Catherine MacBride/Getty; p. 72 (B): Stuart O'Sullivan/Getty; p. 74 (a): anna quaglia/Alamy; p. 74 (b): Arcaid Images/Alamy; p. 74 (c): Larry Lilac/Alamy; p. 74 (d): atm2003/Shutterstock; p. 75 (b): Allison Herreid/Shutterstock; p. 75 (TL): SIMON MAINA/Getty; p. 76: Picade LLC/Alamy; p. 77 (1): Construction Photography/Alamy; p. 77 (2): Lourens Smak/Alamy; p. 77 (3): Kristoffer Tripplaar/Alamy; p. 77 (4): imageBROKER/Alamy; p. 78: Monkey Business Images/Shutterstock; p. 80–81: Colin Anderson/Getty; p. 82 (b/g): Traveller Martin/Shutterstock; p. 82 (1): Anadolu Agency/Getty; p. 82 (2): GABRIEL BOUYS/Getty; p. 82 (3): John Baran/Alamy; p. 82 (4): scibak/Getty; p. 82 (5): Nasa/Corbis; p. 82 (6): Albert Barr/Shutterstock; p. 82 (7): Art Directors & TRIP/Alamy; p. 82 (8): World History Archive/Alamy; p. 82 (9): Redmond Durrell/Alamy; p. 82 (10): Michael Rosskothen/Shutterstock; p. 83 (TL): The Asahi Shimbun/Getty; p. 83 (TM): NASA/Getty; p. 83 (TR): NASA/Getty; p. 83 (BL): Universal Images Group Limited/Alamy; p. 83 (BR): amana images inc./Alamy; p. 84 (BL): Richard T. Nowitz/Corbis; p. 84 (MR): Visions of America, LLC/Alamy; p. 84 (BR): Andrew Kornylak/Corbis; p. 86 (a): Roger Ressmeyer/Corbis; p. 86 (b): Northfoto/Shutterstock; p. 86 (c): NASA Photo/Alamy; p. 86 (d): Ralph Morse/Getty; p. 86 (e): PF-(space1)/Alamy; p. 87: Stocktrek Images, Inc./Alamy; p. 88: Maciej Sojka/Shutterstock; p. 89 (1): Mona/Shutterstock; p. 89 (3): Bill Heinsohn/Alamy; p. 90–91: Nutexzles/Getty; p. 92 (b/g): Nednapa/Getty; p. 92 (1): Jose Lucas/Alamy; p. 92 (2): P Tomlins/Alamy; p. 92 (3): David Gee 4/Alamy; p. 92 (4): Robert Harding World Imagery/Alamy; p. 92 (5): John de la Bastide/Alamy; p. 92 (6): CANARYLUC/Shutterstock; p. 92 (7): Pascal van Heesch/Alamy; p. 92 (8): Jenny Matthews/Alamy; p. 92 (9): Scott Hortop Travel/Alamy; p. 92 (10): solarseven/Shutterstock; p. 93 (1): Hale-Sutton Europe/Alamy; p. 93 (2): David Anthony/Alamy; p. 93 (3): Heritage Image Partnership Ltd/Alamy; p. 93 (4): D. Hurst/Alamy; p. 94 (LT): Kekyalyaynen/Shutterstock; p. 94 (LM): Image Source/Alamy; p. 94 (LB): Lenscap/Alamy; p. 94 (RT): ThreeRivers11/Shutterstock; p. 94 (RM): Lisa F. Young/Shutterstock; p. 94 (RB): Nathaniel Noir/Alamy; p. 96: criben/Shutterstock; p. 97: Gerda Beekers/Shutterstock; p. 98: areeya_ann/Shutterstock; p. 99 (1): Adam J/Shutterstock; p. 99 (2): James Brey/Getty; p. 99 (3): Renata Apanaviciene/Shutterstock; p. 99 (4): Mohammed Anwarul Kabir Choudhury/Alamy. Commissioned photography by Gareth Boden: p. 8 (TR), (B), p. 13 (BR); p. 17; p. 18; p. 23 (BR), p. 28; p. 30; p. 33 (BR); p. 40 (TR); p. 45 (BR); p. 50 (TR); pp. 53–54 (B/G); p. 55 (BR); p. 62 (TR); p. 67 (BR); p. 72 (TR); p. 77 (BR); p. 82; p. 83 (TR, BR); p. 84; p.89 (BR); p.94 (TR); p. 99 (BR).

Additional artwork by: Femke Buitelaar p. 13; p. 55. Naomi Cooper p. 100.

Our special thanks to the following for their kind help during location photography: Coleridge Community College, Parkside Federation Academies

Front Cover photo by aghezzi/Getty Images